ALVIN STEADFAST
ON VERNACULAR ISLAND

ALVIN STEADFAST ON VERNACULAR ISLAND

FRANK JACOBS

DRAWINGS BY EDWARD GOREY

TAPLINGER PUBLISHING COMPANY
New York

For
Alexander

First Taplinger edition 1979

Copyright © 1965, 1979 by Frank Jacobs
Illustrations © 1965, 1979 by Edward Gorey

Library of Congress Catalog Number: 78-20692
ISBN 0-8008-0173-3 (cloth)
ISBN 0-8008-0174-1 (pbk)

Printed in the United States of America

9 8 7 6 5 4 3 2 1

THE ISLAND

The small boat, its sails billowing in the ocean breeze, glided smoothly toward the island.

"We shall be in the cove by noon," said the white-haired man, peering through a small telescope at the approaching land. He was Dr. Thaddeus Cranshaw, the famed scientist and discoverer of more remarkable places and creatures than any other living man.

The person to whom he addressed his remark was Alvin Steadfast, the brilliant ten-year-old explorer, whose skill and daring had earned him the reputation of being the foremost young adventurer of his time. Alvin and Dr. Cranshaw had sailed three thousand miles in their rugged sloop, *The Dauntless*, and were at last reaching their destination, Vernacular Island.

"Making this voyage with you has certainly been a great thrill," Alvin said proudly.

"Nonsense," answered Dr. Cranshaw, who was not a man for sentiment. "Anyway, our work is just beginning. There is much to observe and study on Vernacular Island, which is why I have selected you as my assistant from among more than five hundred applicants. You will remember that the island was my home for more than seven years, and now I am returning to explore its most distant parts."

Alvin looked at the old scientist with friendship and respect. He had been fortunate indeed to be selected from among the five hundred boys who had wished to accompany Dr. Cranshaw on his expedition. But there would be time to think about that later. Now he must help guide the sloop toward the island.

"Steady as she goes," shouted the old scientist.

"Aye, aye, sir," responded Alvin, as the slim craft sailed into the welcoming cove.

After tying up the sloop at the wooden pier, the pair strode onto the sandy shore.

"It is good to be home again," sighed Dr. Cranshaw. "How does the island look to you, Alvin?"

The young explorer gazed around him. Blue ocean waters lapped gently at the white sands of the beach. About one hundred feet away from where they stood, the forest began. There seemed to be many trees and an abundance of tall grass on the island. In the far distance, he could make out three large mountains.

"I like it fine, sir," Alvin said pleasantly. "Shall I start unloading the provisions?"

"That can wait. First we shall have a proper luncheon. Come with me."

They had taken only a few steps up the beach when there was a violent rustling of foliage. The young explorer looked toward the forest. Racing through the trees and approaching the beach was a sleek deerlike creature. It was white with bright red streaks extending from its neck to its tail. It galloped very fast, and as it got nearer Alvin could hear it bellow out.

"The boat has landed. Yes, the boat has landed and Doctor Cranshaw has returned to Vernacular Island. He has brought with him a young explorer named Alvin. That is all for now. I shall be back to relate future events just as soon as they happen." The creature made several wide circles around Dr. Cranshaw and Alvin, then galloped back into the forest.

"What was that?" the boy asked.

"That," explained the old scientist, "was the Running Commentary."

"The Running Commentary?" asked Alvin.

"Yes. You will most likely see him again. He lives in the forest, but spends nearly all of his time racing around the island. He keeps me posted on what is going on throughout Vernacular. Oh, oh, here he comes again."

The Running Commentary burst once more through the trees and began racing around the beach.

"Here I am again," the creature bellowed, "to relate an item of awful news. The Doubt is in the mountains. I repeat—the Doubt is in the mountains. That is all for now. I shall be back to relate future events just as soon as they happen." The Running Commentary made one last circle and sped back into the forest.

"What did he mean about a doubt in the mountains?" asked Alvin.

"It means trouble," said Dr. Cranshaw, shaking his head in dismay. "We have arrived not a moment too soon."

"Are we going to put an end to the doubt in the mountains?" asked the young explorer, who was looking forward to a time of great adventure.

"Of course, my boy, of course," said the old scientist. "We shall discuss it after luncheon."

"Where?" asked Alvin.

"At my home in the clearing. Follow me."

THE WELCOME

Alvin and Dr. Cranshaw walked up the beach and through a patch of jungle brush. Abruptly they were in a great clearing. In the center of the open space was a large, sprawling house. The boy was about to compliment the scientist on the splendor of the house when the calm of the clearing was shattered by very loud clapping. Alvin looked toward the house; two creatures were coming out the front door.

The first was an elegant being about four feet tall. His body was coated with a layer of light blue scales arranged in a handsome design, and he glittered in the sun as he strode through the clearing. His face was graced by refined features: clear blue eyes, a broad smile of appreciation, and a splendid moustache that was neatly trimmed. He walked slowly, majestically, his hands clutching a tray containing two empty glasses and what appeared to be some sandwiches.

The second creature, who was considerably taller than the first, followed several feet behind.

11

Although he was not as elegant, he was certainly as noticeable. Except for his face, his entire body was covered with a rich coat of orange fur. As he approached Alvin and Dr. Cranshaw, he marched a few steps, stopped, stood at attention, and clapped his hands furiously. Then he marched a few more steps and clapped some more.

"Gosh," Alvin murmured, "who are they?"

"I will introduce you," said Dr. Cranshaw, leading the boy toward the first creature. The second one had stopped to applaud so many times that he had fallen far behind.

"Alvin, I would like you to meet the Appropriate Gesture."

"I'm very pleased to meet you," said Alvin, whereupon the Appropriate Gesture bowed low and spoke in a deep, resonant voice.

"I am honored, sir, and won't you be so kind as to have a planter's punch and a cream cheese sandwich?"

Alvin was rather surprised by the offer, since the glasses on the tray did not contain planter's punch. In fact, since they were empty, they did not contain anything at all. What was more, there were no cream cheese sandwiches on the tray, only some slices of bread with nothing in between.

Alvin hesitated, but Dr. Cranshaw whispered in his ear, "Take them. He'll be offended if you don't."

Alvin selected one of the empty glasses and two of the slices of bread and thanked the Appropriate Gesture.

"Not at all, sir," the creature replied. "A pleasure to serve you." He then turned to Dr. Cranshaw, who also took an empty glass and two slices of bread. "Will that be all, sir?" the creature asked.

"Yes," said the old scientist. "You may go now, and take the rest of the day off."

"Very good, sir. Thank you, sir. But I shall remain close by should you require my services."

"How unusual!" exclaimed Alvin as he watched the Appropriate Gesture head back toward the house. "He certainly is considerate."

"Yes, he is," said Dr. Cranshaw. "You must understand that the Appropriate Gesture does everything he can to live up to his name. When he saw us approaching the house, he immediately decided that we were hungry and thirsty and so filled his tray."

"But he didn't put anything in the glasses or anything between the bread," said Alvin.

"Oh, he is never concerned about such details. To him it is the gesture that counts, and if it is appropriate, so much the better. You will admit that bringing us refreshments was an appropriate gesture."

"Yes, but . . ."

"Then that is all that counts, isn't it?"

Alvin wanted to pursue the subject further, but his thoughts were diverted by the second creature, who was now standing at attention only a few feet from them and clapping so loudly that the noise prevented anyone from speaking.

Dr. Cranshaw allowed the applause to continue

for several seconds, then raised his hand as a signal for the clapping to stop. The creature placed his arms at his sides, but continued to stand at attention, his bright orange fur contrasting vividly with the green of the grass. Alvin could not help but be impressed by the creature's height; he was over seven feet tall, and his fine posture made him seem even taller.

Once again, Alvin was introduced.

"This," said Dr. Cranshaw, "is the Standing Ovation."

The creature beamed proudly as he heard his name spoken.

"Each time I cross the clearing he is here to welcome me with his splendid greeting," the old scientist continued. "Although he has applauded me more than a thousand times, I still have the same feeling of gratification each time it happens."

Dr. Cranshaw's last remark somehow served as a signal for the Standing Ovation to begin clapping again. The applause was furious. It echoed through the clearing, and Alvin was convinced it could be heard at least three miles away. After a few moments, Dr. Cranshaw raised his hand to stop the applause. This time, however, the creature was not to be stopped. Remaining at attention and smiling directly at Dr. Cranshaw, he continued his thunderous clapping despite the old scientist's efforts to end it.

"That is enough!" Dr. Cranshaw cried, but the clapping did not stop. "Confound it!" shouted the old scientist, cupping his hands and shouting to

Alvin, "but why must he overdo it so? I cannot stand such emotional scenes!"

It was clear to Alvin that nothing Dr. Cranshaw did would stop the Standing Ovation. Therefore, the young explorer pointed toward the house.

"Capital idea!" yelled Dr. Cranshaw. "We shall go inside."

Leaving the Standing Ovation at the edge of the clearing, the pair headed toward the house, the applause still booming in their ears. Alvin wondered how long the creature would keep applauding, but he didn't ask. Dr. Cranshaw was obviously distressed, and the boy did not wish to upset him more. Anyway, they would soon be having luncheon, and Alvin hoped it would calm the old scientist's nerves.

16

THE GLOWING REPORT

Alvin and Dr. Cranshaw were sitting outside the house relaxing after a most enjoyable luncheon. The boy was happy to note that the old scientist had recovered from his attack of nerves and was back to his normal self.

"Would you care for another mango?" Dr. Cranshaw asked, offering Alvin a bowl of the delicious yellow fruit.

"No, sir, but now that we have finished our luncheon, I have a question. You have not as yet told me how we are going to put an end to the doubt in the mountains. What is a doubt, anyway?"

The old scientist stopped slicing his mango, then furled his brow and bowed his head in deep thought. After several moments, he raised his head and looked Alvin square in the eye.

"My boy," he said softly, "I haven't the foggiest idea."

"But, sir," said Alvin, "how shall we ever put an end to the doubt if we don't know what a doubt is?"

Dr. Cranshaw shook his head. "I have been tracking the Doubt for years," he said. "I have looked for him all over this island—on the beaches, in the forests, in the swamps—but I have never found him. There is only one place I haven't looked."

"The mountains!" exclaimed Alvin.

"Precisely," answered the old scientist. "But I could not explore the mountains until I had the services of an assistant, and that is why you are here."

Alvin's eyes brightened. He was prouder than ever to be able to serve the old scientist.

"The Doubt," explained Dr. Cranshaw, "is a clever creature, as cunning as he is evil. Tracking him down will require the utmost skill and daring and may even call on our innermost resources. The area we shall explore is untouched by man. I do not know what we shall find. I do not even know if we shall return."

Alvin was immensely pleased. He had hoped that his work would prove interesting. Now it was proving to be not only interesting, but exciting and dangerous as well.

"And now let us get down to business," Dr. Cranshaw said, whereupon he picked up a large iron bell from the table and rang it furiously. It summoned two creatures, neither of whom Alvin had ever met before.

"Ah!" said Dr. Cranshaw. "The Glowing Report!"

"Good afternoon, Doctor Cranshaw," exclaimed

the Glowing Report. He was a square-shaped fellow whose skin glowed yellow-green. Alvin noticed that each time he spoke his glow turned into a blinding glare. In fact, it was because of the glare that the young explorer almost missed the entrance of the other, smaller visitor, who had followed the Glowing Report onto the terrace.

The smaller creature was also extraordinary. He was about a foot tall and had six arms. His color appeared to be brown; it was difficult for Alvin to judge exactly because everything on the terrace was now bathed in the yellow-green glare of the Glowing Report.

The little creature moved very quickly, hopping from chair to table, stacking up the luncheon dishes with one hand, rolling up the tablecloth with another, collecting the silverware with another. In a few seconds he had completely cleared the table. Then, balancing all of the dishes, silverware, glasses, and linens on his arms, he jumped off the table and carried everything down the hall to the kitchen.

"Who was that?" wondered Alvin aloud.

"The Small Wonder," said Dr. Cranshaw. "Remarkable little fellow, isn't he? Never wastes a motion. He keeps the entire house shipshape—and all by himself, too. Clears the table, washes the dishes, waxes the floors, polishes the windows—often all at the same time."

"Can he take out the garbage as well?" asked Alvin, who was a firm believer in all kinds of cleanliness.

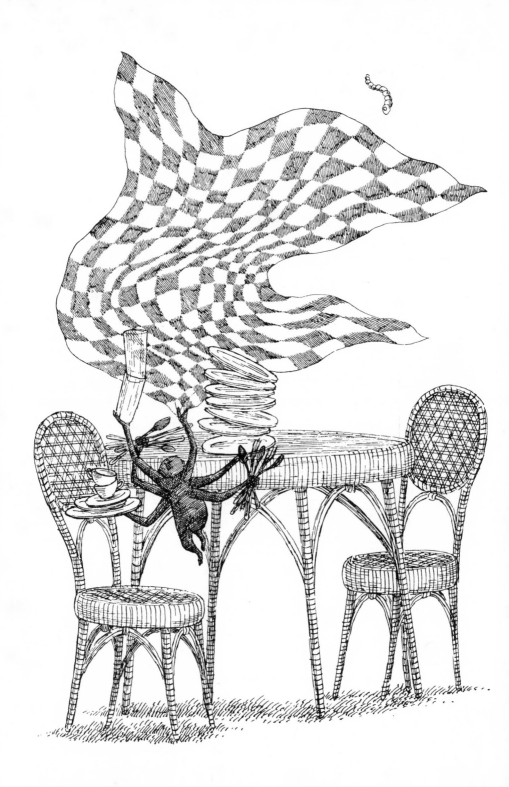

The old scientist, however, had turned his attention to the Glowing Report, who was glimmering softly in the corner.

"Now that I have returned to Vernacular Island," Dr. Cranshaw addressed the creature, "I trust you are ready to deliver your report."

"Bless my soul, yes!" exclaimed the Glowing Report in his high-pitched voice. "I know you'll simply *love* it!"

"Very well, then," said the old scientist, taking a leather-bound notebook out of his pocket. "Report."

The Glowing Report cleared his throat, the brief sound flooding the terrace in a sea of yellow-green light. Then striking a dramatic pose, he began reporting. "I just so *adore* being here," he glowed, "and I have the most *divine* report to make. I'll begin by letting you in on a little secret. I wouldn't want it to go any farther, but today is the *marvelous* day of Tuesday!"

Alvin saw that a frown was forming on Dr. Cranshaw's face. However, the Glowing Report did not seem to notice and continued reporting.

"In addition," the creature went on, "it is now the simply *wonderful* hour of two o'clock."

The frown on Dr. Cranshaw's face was now turning into a scowl, and Alvin noted that the old scientist had not written any of the report in his notebook.

"He is obviously displeased," Alvin said to himself.

"Is this the best you can do?" Dr. Cranshaw inquired sternly. "I have been gone for more than a year, and I expect you to tell me what has happened during my absence."

The Glowing Report nodded and continued.

"The island has been simply heavenly! I mean, the sun has been too *gorgeous* for words, shining like a beautiful jewel on the *dazzling* ocean!"

As he finished the sentence, the Glowing Report smiled sweetly at Dr. Cranshaw. The old scientist, however, was now scowling fiercely.

"I don't care about the ocean!" he shouted. "I want to know about the Doubt and what he's been up to!"

The Glowing Report continued as if he had not heard Dr. Cranshaw.

"Each morning," the creature went on, "there's been just a *hint* of rain, and I don't have to tell you that the grass and flowers simply love it!"

As the Glowing Report made this last statement, he worked up his grandest glow of the day. He was obviously in good form because his yellow-green glare was more dazzling than any light Alvin had ever seen. It flooded the terrace and even spread several hundred feet into the clearing.

"There has been joy!" exclaimed the creature at the peak of his glow. "Joy and happiness and sweetness and pleasure and happiness and joy and delight and sweetness and happiness and . . ."

"Enough!" thundered Dr. Cranshaw, flailing his arms at the Glowing Report. "I need to know of

the Doubt, and you talk of joy! Go! Leave at once and do not return until you have learned to prepare a report that is useful!"

The creature glowed brightly. "I am so pleased to have helped," he said, backing off and disappearing into the house.

Dr. Cranshaw sat gloomily, shaking his head. "I should have learned by now," he muttered, "that a Glowing Report is never very helpful."

"What is next on the schedule for today?" asked Alvin, hoping that his question would help the old scientist forget his disappointment.

"Next, my boy," said Dr. Cranshaw, "we must unload the provisions from the boat. Then it is off to bed early, because at dawn tomorrow we begin our journey to the mountain regions, which are fraught with danger and peril. How does that sound to you?"

"Fine, sir," Alvin said breathlessly, looking at the distant peaks. How wonderful it was, he thought to himself, that he and Dr. Cranshaw would be the first men ever to go there. And how even more wonderful that they might never return.

THE SAFARI

Dawn found Alvin and Dr. Cranshaw in the clearing. They had enjoyed a hearty breakfast and were setting up their safari for the journey to the mountain regions, which they hoped to reach by early afternoon.

While Alvin studied a large map of the island, the old scientist busied himself lining up the safari. There would be five members in the expedition, and each of them would have his own special duties to perform.

Leading the explorers, of course, was Dr. Cranshaw, splendidly attired in a white uniform and pith helmet. He wore polished black boots that came almost up to his knees. Around his neck were slung a pair of binoculars and a policeman's whistle, and in his pocket were a compass and his leather-bound notebook.

Just behind Dr. Cranshaw was a very thin blue-and-white creature with a long, sharp beak, long legs, and pointed feet. He was the Conditioned

Reflex, and it would be his job to warn the safari in case of trouble. His eyes were very large, and he had the odd habit of turning his head from one direction to another every five seconds.

In the number three position was the Ultimate Aim. He was a roly-poly little fellow with sharp, squinting eyes and thin lips. Although his head was white, his body was spotted with black polka dots. Unlike the Conditioned Reflex, the Ultimate Aim always kept his eyes straight ahead. It would be up to him to make sure that the expedition reached the mountain regions in the shortest possible time.

Next was the Common Good. He was tall, bulky, and friendly, but other than that he was not easy to describe. He wasn't particularly handsome, but he wasn't particularly ugly, either. He was just a plain-looking creature who believed there was good in everyone. The Common Good was a very important member of the safari since he carried all of the provisions on his back. At the moment, his color was soft yellow, but he changed it at will, depending on whom he was talking to and how good he felt.

The fifth and final member of the safari was, of course, Alvin. The young explorer was dressed in a white uniform, similar to that worn by Dr. Cranshaw, except that he scorned a pith helmet and wore a broad-brimmed hat instead. Like the old scientist, Alvin also wore black boots and carried a pair of binoculars around his neck.

Finally the members of the safari were all lined up and ready to depart. Dr. Cranshaw turned from his position at the front of the line and called to Alvin.

"Ready at the fore!"

Alvin shouted back.

"Ready at the rear!"

"Very well, then," announced the old scientist proudly, whereupon he blew a long blast on his policeman's whistle and called out the long-awaited command.

"Onward!"

The safari entered the forest and had traveled almost a mile when Dr. Cranshaw shouted, "Halt!"

Alvin was very surprised. He could think of no reason why they should be stopping. However, the narrow path curved so greatly that he could not see to the front of the safari. There must be some obstacle in our path, he thought. The young explorer inched his way up the trail, squeezing around the other members of the safari, until he reached Dr. Cranshaw.

The old scientist was leaning dejectedly against a tree.

"This will never do. This will never do at all," he moaned as Alvin reached his side. "Just take a look."

NATURAL ENEMIES

Alvin looked ahead and was amazed at what he saw.

Blocking the trail were two large, fierce birds. The first was rust-colored with green, piercing eyes, long teeth, and a sullen expression. The second was completely purple. Its tongue was stuck out at the first bird, and it glowered hatefully. The two birds faced each other. They did not speak and they did not move, but simply glared in dark silence.

"Who are they?" the young explorer asked.

"The Bitter Grudge and the Purple Rage," Dr. Cranshaw answered, removing his pith helmet and wiping his brow.

"Why won't they fly out of our way?" Alvin inquired.

"Because they hate each other so much that they don't care about anything else."

"Won't they move if we ask them?"

"It is useless to reason with them. They are obstinate, stupid creatures. However, you may try if you wish."

Alvin approached the Bitter Grudge carefully, as it was obvious that the bird was mean and dangerous.

"Won't you please fly away so we can travel through?" he asked.

"*I* would not mind moving," answered the Bitter Grudge without taking his eyes off his enemy, "but he won't."

"Have you asked him to move?" inquired Alvin.

"Of course not," said the Grudge. "We're not speaking."

Alvin then turned to the Purple Rage. "Why aren't you two speaking?" he asked.

"Because we are natural enemies," answered the Purple Rage.

"Why are you natural enemies?"

"Because we hate each other."

"Why do you hate each other?"

"Because we're not speaking."

"Why aren't you speaking?"

"Because we are natural enemies. Can't you understand English?"

Alvin had to admit to himself that there was some sense to what the Purple Rage said. Still, it all seemed so unnecessary.

"Can't we do anything about them?" he asked Dr. Cranshaw.

"Confound it all, but we *must* do something!" shouted the old scientist, throwing his pith helmet against a tree. "But I can't for the life of me think what!"

"Let me try," murmured a very, very slow, deep voice from the rear.

Dr. Cranshaw turned his head. "Who said that?"

"I did," said the Common Good, squeezing his way past the Ultimate Aim and the Conditioned Reflex.

"Do you really think you can get those two hooligans out of our way?" Dr. Cranshaw asked.

"I think I can," murmured the Common Good, who did not appear the least bit tired despite the fact that he had been carrying all of the safari's provisions on his back.

"Why not let him try?" inquired Alvin of Dr. Cranshaw.

The old scientist shook his head.

"A thorny problem, my boy," he whispered. "If we do not clear the path, we shall have to turn back. On the other hand, if the Common Good is hurt, then we shall have no one to carry our provisions, and we shall still have to turn back. Ah, but look! He is beginning to change."

Alvin looked. Sure enough, the Common Good was changing his color from a soft yellow to a pale off-white. "What does it mean, sir?" the boy asked.

"Whenever the Common Good is preparing to do something for the benefit of mankind, he becomes a pale off-white. It is a glorious thing to behold."

The Common Good stood before Dr. Cranshaw. "Can I help now?" the creature asked.

"Are you sure you feel up to it?" countered the old scientist.

"Oh yes," said the creature. "I am good, good, good."

"Very well, then," said Dr. Cranshaw, "but be careful."

The Common Good nodded his head. After removing the provisions from his back, he trod slowly toward the narrow part of the trail where the Bitter Grudge and the Purple Rage were facing each other.

"Good . . . good . . . good," he muttered as he approached the natural enemies. The Grudge and the Rage were so engrossed in their scowling that they did not notice the Common Good until he was just a foot away.

"Good . . . good . . . good," he continued muttering.

The two angry birds looked up and snarled, as if they were about to attack the Common Good with their sharp beaks. But they were too late. Before they could do anything at all, the Common Good stretched out his huge hands and picked them up by the scruffs of their necks.

"Good . . . good . . . good," he muttered, gripping their necks firmly.

"No! No! No!" they screamed, struggling to claw him.

"Good . . . good . . . good," he repeated, tightening his grip even more.

"No! No! No!" they screeched, trying to bite him.

"Good . . . good . . . good," he persisted, gripping their necks so tightly that they couldn't breathe.

"Oh, yes, yes, yes," the birds gasped as they stopped their vicious struggling. "We will be good, good, good forever, forever, forever."

The Common Good smiled, nodded his head, and let go of their necks. Exhausted, the birds spread their wings and had just strength left to flutter onto the branches of a nearby tree.

Alvin, who had been watching with great interest, hoped that the birds' quarrel was ended completely. "Do you think the Bitter Grudge and the Purple Rage will ever be enemies again?" he asked Dr. Cranshaw.

"Not a chance of it, my boy," answered the old scientist. "They have reformed for the Common Good."

"That is heartwarming news," said Alvin, who then excused himself to take his place at the rear of the safari. Now that the path was cleared, the expedition could begin moving again. One by one, the members fell in step behind Dr. Cranshaw.

From his rear position, Alvin glanced back at the spot where the angry birds had blocked the path. He was very surprised at what he saw. The Bitter Grudge and the Purple Rage had flown down from their perches. Once again they were facing each other in the middle of the trail with hate in their eyes. The young explorer watched the angry, silent birds for a moment, wondering if he should tell Dr. Cranshaw about them. He decided not to.

It might shake the old scientist's faith in the Common Good, and that was something Alvin did not want to do. Anyway, there was much hard work ahead, and they would have to march briskly if they were to reach the mountain regions by early afternoon.

THE ILL OMEN

"We would have arrived by now if we had gone far enough," said the Ultimate Aim, his roly-poly polka dot body gleaming in the midday sun.

The safari had traveled through the forest and now was resting in a green meadow. Not too far off were the mountains toward which they were heading. The other members of the expedition had gathered around the Ultimate Aim and were listening intently.

"If we keep up our current rate of travel," the Aim continued, "we shall walk as far in the next hour as we have in the one just gone by."

"Splendid!" exclaimed Dr. Cranshaw, raising his binoculars to his eyes. "Can you tell us how far away we are from the mountains?"

"According to my calculations," said the Ultimate Aim, "we are not far away at all. We are close by."

"I thought as much," said the old scientist, peering through his binoculars at the rugged peaks.

"Which mountain, do you suppose, is the home of the Doubt?"

Before the Ultimate Aim could answer, a wild shriek was heard. It was followed by a loud yapping. "It's true! It's true! They're talking about it all over the forest! The Ultimate Aim is an idiot who can't find his way!"

Alvin looked around to see who could be saying such a terrible thing, because he knew that the Ultimate Aim was the best guide an expedition could possibly have.

The yapping continued.

"It's true! It's true! Everybody's saying it. The Ultimate Aim is so dense that he couldn't find his way out of a closet!"

At last Alvin discovered the source of the noise. Sunning itself on a large rock was a long snakelike creature with a green scaly body and an enormous mouth. It was a slithery animal, and it made a disgusting clicking sound with its teeth when it wasn't yapping.

"What is that?" asked the young explorer.

"An Ugly Rumor," said Dr. Cranshaw, attempting to seize the creature by its tail. It darted away before the old scientist could catch it.

"One fact is all too true," he said, watching the creature disappear into its hole. "No matter how hard we try, we can never pin down an Ugly Rumor."

No one in the safari, of course, believed a word of what the Ugly Rumor said. However, the creature's vicious attack had greatly upset the Ultimate

39

Aim, who now sat dejectedly beneath a bush. Fortunately, his gloom did not last long, mainly because of the efforts of the Common Good, who consoled him, telling him over and over that he was the best guide in the whole world.

Dr. Cranshaw, meanwhile, sat on an old board stuck in the ground and studied his maps.

"I must find out which mountain is the home of the Doubt," he murmured to himself.

"Begging your pardon, sir," said Alvin, who had been standing close by with an eager expression on his face.

"Don't bother me now, my boy," said Dr. Cranshaw.

"But, sir . . ."

"Later, my boy, later."

"But I think I know where you can get the information you are seeking."

"And how would you know that?"

"Because," Alvin said, "there is an information booth ahead."

"An information booth? What makes you think that?"

"Because of the sign, sir, on which you are sitting."

Dr. Cranshaw raised himself and looked down. It was true. He had been sitting on a wooden sign, and it said

INFORMATION BOOTH AHEAD

"We must go there immediately," the old scientist declared.

"Yes, sir," responded Alvin, feeling quite proud that he had been of some service. "Perhaps it will not be too far away."

"Information booth directly ahead," shouted the Ultimate Aim, once again his old self.

"Excellent!" exclaimed Dr. Cranshaw, pushing forward. He saw that there was a large sign on a wooden shack that said

INFORMATION BOOTH

Beneath it, however, was another sign that said

Closed on Account of Illness

Dr. Cranshaw threw his pith helmet to the ground.

"Just our luck!" he wailed. "Now we shall never find out which mountain is the home of the Doubt."

Just then there came the faint sound of someone coughing.

"Who was that?" asked the old scientist.

"It was I," answered a weak voice. "Over here. Behind the information booth."

Dr. Cranshaw and Alvin peered behind the booth. There they discovered a thin, gray, furry creature resting in a hammock.

"Good afternoon," it coughed.

"Good afternoon," responded Dr. Cranshaw with a polite nod. "We are looking for the person who runs the information booth."

"I run the information booth," said the creature, wiping his nose with a red handkerchief.

"And who are you, if I may ask?"

"I am an omen."

"Why are you resting in this hammock and not minding the information booth?"

"I had to close the information booth because I am not feeling well," sniffed the creature. "You see, I am an ill omen."

"Of course," said Dr. Cranshaw, for it was clear that the omen was not at all well. "Just what seems to be ailing you?"

"I have a cold," murmured the creature.

"How long have you been feeling this way?" asked the old scientist.

"For seventeen years."

"Isn't seventeen years a long time to have a cold?"

"Yes, but I believe in letting it run its course."

"Are you keeping warm, getting plenty of rest, and drinking lots of liquids?" interjected Alvin, who always did these things when he had a cold.

"Most certainly," answered the Ill Omen, sneezing quietly. "How else will I ever get well?"

"Yes, yes, yes," Dr. Cranshaw said, somewhat impatiently, "but I am afraid that we do not have the time to discuss your illness. You see, I had hoped you might impart some information."

"Oh, please let me try and help you," coughed the creature. "You are the first customers I have had since I was taken ill."

"Very well," said the old scientist. "I am leading a safari to explore the mountain regions, and I wish to know which of the three mountains is the home of the Doubt."

"I can answer that," said the Ill Omen. "The Doubt lives on the mountain in the middle, but I would not go there if I were you."

"And why not?" asked Dr. Cranshaw.

"Because of what I shall now tell you," coughed the creature. Then he propped himself up on one elbow and recited the following verse:

"Beware the shadow of a Doubt;
It finds your fears and brings them out.
You cannot fight or run away;
And that is all I have to say."

The Ill Omen then coughed twice, lurched back, and fell soundly asleep.

"A meaningless rhyme," Dr. Cranshaw shrugged.

"Does it not worry you?" Alvin asked earnestly, for he had been truly impressed by the creature's verse.

"Fiddle-faddle!" snorted the old scientist. "This

is no time to be superstitious. It is a sorry day when we become frightened of Ill Omens."

"Then we are still going to explore the mountain in the middle?"

"Of course, my boy. After all, we owe it to the world of science. Now let us be off."

"Yes, sir," Alvin answered obediently. Deep in his heart, though, the young explorer was concerned. He was not afraid, but he did feel that there was some unknown danger ahead and that they should be most cautious. However, he did not wish to argue with Dr. Cranshaw. The old scientist had chosen him for this expedition from among more than five hundred applicants, and it would be impolite to dispute him.

"I must keep silent," Alvin said to himself, "even though I feel some awful peril awaits us on the road ahead."

THE CAPTURE

It was one-thirty in the afternoon when the safari reached the foot of the middle mountain.

"Halt!" shouted Dr. Cranshaw. "We will rest here for ten minutes."

Then, suddenly, the Conditioned Reflex, who had been dozing, rose and sniffed the air.

"I smell trouble," he declared, jerking his head twice.

No sooner had his words been spoken than something very unusual happened.

A strange dark shadow fell over Dr. Cranshaw.

One reason the shadow was strange was that it fell over Dr. Cranshaw and nobody else. It made no difference where the old scientist moved; the shadow followed him. But even more strange was the way the shadow affected Dr. Cranshaw's mind. A moment before, he had been a brave, strong, confident leader. Now he seemed frightened and unsure of himself. He walked around in circles, shaking his head and muttering sad things. "We are doomed," Alvin could hear Dr. Cranshaw saying. "We are all eternally, infernally doomed."

The young explorer was puzzled. What was the strange, dark shadow that had cast its awful spell on Dr. Cranshaw? He looked to the sky, and there he discovered the terrible answer.

Hovering high over Dr. Cranshaw was a monstrous flying beast. It was not a real bird, but it was not an animal either. It had a head like a lizard and great batlike wings that measured twenty feet across. It was completely black, and whenever it breathed there was a hideous low wheeze.

Alvin watched in amazement as the creature hovered directly over Dr. Cranshaw. The huge beast maneuvered carefully so that no matter where the old scientist stood he was always in its shadow.

"Woe, woe, woe," moaned Dr. Cranshaw, still wandering around in circles. "It is just as I feared. There is no hope. The expedition is doomed. We have failed."

"How remarkable!" Alvin said to himself. "Earlier Dr. Cranshaw was brave and confident, but now he is filled with fear."

Then, in a flash, Alvin realized what was happening. He thought back to the meeting with the Ill Omen and the rhyme that the creature had spoken. *Beware the shadow of a Doubt; it finds your fears and brings them out.* The rhyme explained everything. The shadow of a Doubt had fallen over Dr. Cranshaw!

So that is what a Doubt looks like, Alvin thought.

Alvin looked at the ugly black beast hovering overhead. Perhaps if he threw stones at it, it would fly away. It would do no harm to try, in any case. But before Alvin could act, the Doubt swooped down.

"Too late—heef, heef—too late," it wheezed. "You can't stop me," and with that the beast flew straight for Dr. Cranshaw. Holding the old scientist's collar tightly in its beak, it flapped its wings and flew off toward the top of the mountain.

From the ground, Alvin could hear Dr. Cranshaw moaning as he was carried through the air.

"We are utterly lost," he cried. "There is no hope at all."

Alvin cupped his hands and shouted as loud as he could.

"Do not give up, sir! I shall save you from the awful beast!" But deep in his heart Alvin knew that a rescue would be very difficult. Dr. Cranshaw, alas, had been seized by a Doubt!

The young explorer watched through his binoculars as the hideous creature flew to the very top of the mountain. The Doubt circled the uppermost crag, then flew onto its nest, taking the old scientist with him. "Poor Doctor Cranshaw," muttered Alvin, "held prisoner of such a terrible creature! What on earth can we do to save him?"

The Ultimate Aim proposed that they climb straight up the mountain and kill the Doubt. That was not a good plan, Alvin pointed out, because the beast could simply pick up Dr. Cranshaw and fly off to one of the other mountains.

The Conditioned Reflex put forth the idea that they build a large catapult and hurl rocks up at the Doubt. Alvin explained that the rocks might miss the beast and strike Dr. Cranshaw.

The Common Good suggested that he be allowed to tear down the mountain piece by piece. This idea, too, was turned down after Alvin calculated that it would take the Common Good two hundred and twenty-five years to accomplish such a task.

No, they must come up with a better idea. The Doubt was obviously a clever creature, and it would require an exceptional plan to outwit it. But what kind of plan?

After several moments of thought, Alvin had an idea. He called together the other members of the safari.

"I have a plan to save our noble leader," he told them. "If we all work together, it may very well prove successful."

"I shall be proud to assist," said the Conditioned Reflex.

"You can count on me," said the Ultimate Aim.

"I shall do my best," said the Common Good.

"Very well, then," said Alvin. "Here is what we must do . . ."

ALVIN'S PLAN

When the other members of the safari heard Alvin's plan, they were most eager to get started.

"What must be done first?" inquired the Common Good.

"First," said Alvin, "we must paint a sign on the ground that will be big enough for the Doubt to see from his perch at the top of the mountain."

Within a few moments, the Common Good, who carried all of the provisions, had opened the box containing the white paint. Then they all set to work painting a large sign on the ground. It was hard work, and it took the faithful crew almost an hour to complete it. The words had to be very big, each letter ten feet high. But at last the sign was finished. It read

Leading away from the sign were several arrows, which pointed into a nearby clump of trees.

As soon as the sign and arrows were painted, Alvin directed everyone to hide behind a large rock. Then, using his binoculars, the young explorer peered up at the Doubt, who was crouched on its nest high atop the mountain.

Alvin hoped mightily that the Doubt would see the sign. Else the young explorer's plan would go for naught.

Finally, after what seemed a very long time, Alvin saw the Doubt look down. There was a puzzled expression on the beast's face, and he appeared to be fluttering his huge batlike wings.

"I do believe he has seen the sign!" exclaimed Alvin to the Common Good, who was standing nearby.

"But why the sign?" asked the Common Good.

"It is all very simple. We must lure the Doubt away from his perch in order to rescue Doctor Cranshaw. To accomplish this, we have painted this sign which tells of the One Last Hope. Everyone knows that in order for a doubt to survive it must destroy every hope, especially the last one."

"But just what kind of creature is the One Last Hope?" asked the Conditioned Reflex. "I know that I have never seen one."

"Nobody has," explained Alvin, "but the Doubt doesn't know that. We must trust that he believes in signs."

"And what if he *does* believe our sign?"

"Then he most likely will fly down and investigate."

"And then?"

"Then the Doubt will try to find the One Last Hope and destroy him. If all goes well, the Doubt will follow the arrows which lead into that clump of trees. Then, while he is searching, we can scale the mountain and rescue Doctor Cranshaw."

"I think the Doubt is getting ready to fly," said the Conditioned Reflex, whose eyesight was very keen even without binoculars.

"Yes, he is taking off now," said Alvin. "It is most important that the beast does not see us. We must crouch very low behind this rock."

The young explorer and his comrades crouched as low as they could. High above them, the Doubt flapped his monstrous wings and began his downward flight. So powerful was the beast that he reached the painted sign in only a few seconds.

The giant creature hovered a few feet over the sign, examining it carefully. Then he saw the arrows pointing toward the clump of trees. The Doubt fluttered over to the first arrow and examined it just as carefully as he had the sign.

From his hiding place, which was only a few feet away from the sign, Alvin could hear the creature's hideous wheeze.

"The One Last Hope—heef, heef—must be destroyed," it breathed.

As the wheezes of the Doubt grew fainter, Alvin realized that the creature was following the arrows that led to the clump of trees. Finally, the wheezes could not be heard at all.

"If my calculations are correct," Alvin said to himself, "the Doubt should now be entering the forest." The young explorer raised himself just enough to peer over the rock. Sure enough, the creature had touched ground, folded its wings, and headed into the trees.

Alvin waited a few moments to make sure that the Doubt was in the forest. Then, motioning the others to follow him, he left the safety of the rock and started up the mountain.

Fortunately, the mountain was not too steep. Nevertheless, the climbing was not easy. But since the Doubt was still in the forest, Alvin felt there was a good chance that they would be able to reach Dr. Cranshaw before the beast returned.

The young explorer, who was leading the rescuers, climbed farther and farther up the mountain until he was only a few feet from his goal.

"I must not stop now," Alvin said to himself even though he was growing tired from the climbing. And so, redoubling his energies, he scaled the final few feet until he reached the nest of the Doubt at the top of the mountain.

"Doctor Cranshaw, where are you?" he called as he raised himself over the final rocky crag.

"Over here, my boy," came a weak but familiar voice.

Alvin rushed over to the old scientist, who was reclining against a large boulder.

"Are you all right?" asked the boy.

"This has been a harrowing experience," answered Dr. Cranshaw, "and it has taxed my strength. But other than that, I am no worse for wear."

"That is heartwarming news," exclaimed Alvin. "Do not despair any longer, sir. I shall soon have you out of this."

"Oh, no you won't!" wheezed a sinister voice from overhead.

Alvin felt a cold chill creep up his spine, as if the sun had gone behind a cloud, but the young explorer knew that what he felt was not caused by any cloud. It was all too frighteningly clear what had happened.

The Doubt had returned, and Alvin was in its shadow.

THE FINAL OUTCOME

Alvin looked up. The Doubt was hovering over him, its huge ugly body blocking out the sun. The young explorer was in the worst spot of his brilliant career. The other rescuers were still many feet below, and it would take several minutes for them to reach the top. Poor Dr. Cranshaw was so weak from his ordeal that he could do nothing but moan in despair. Escape was impossible. Alvin would have to face the beast alone.

The Doubt leered down, its huge outstretched wings barely moving in the air.

"You tried to trick me," it wheezed at Alvin, "but—heef, heef—I was wise to you from the first. Your sign and arrows did not fool me for a minute, but I let you think they did. And now, reckless lad, you have outsmarted yourself."

Alvin struggled to think of a way out of his terrible dilemma, and as he did he suddenly had a strange realization. *He wasn't frightened.* He knew he was supposed to be, because the shadow of a doubt always brought out a person's fears. Alvin, however, felt no fear at all because he had none to begin with.

"The beast thinks I am frightened," the young explorer said to himself, "and I shall let him think it." The boy thereupon hung his head woefully and muttered, "Alas, I am doomed. There is no chance at all. I am utterly lost and defeated."

The Doubt's face twisted into an evil smile.

"Of course you are doomed," he wheezed, as he descended upon his intended victim, "and now—heef, heef—I shall destroy you."

The beast plunged down at Alvin, but the young explorer deftly stepped aside before it could strike. The creature crashed against a rock.

"How can this be?" it wheezed dazedly. "You are supposed to be too frightened to outwit me. Where are your fears?"

"I have none," Alvin said calmly, looking the Doubt straight in the eye, "and now it is time to see just how awful you really are."

And with that the young explorer grabbed one of the creature's wings.

"No! You must not do that!" cried the beast, cringing. "I meant no harm! Really I didn't!"

But Alvin gave the wing a sharp tug, and he was not surprised when it came off. Then he took hold of the other wing and it, too, came off with little effort.

"I thought as much!" he declared. "Your wings are not real, and I'll wager the rest of you isn't, either."

"Oh, no, please stop!" blubbered the Doubt. "I was just fooling, really I was!"

"There is nothing real about you at all," the boy said confidently, gripping the Doubt by the beak. Once more he pulled, and this time the entire huge head and body of the creature came off. "A false head and a false body as well!"

Its disguise removed, the Doubt stood trembling before the young explorer. It could now be seen for what it really was—a tiny gray creature no bigger than a groundhog.

"How humiliating!" it cried. "Oh, look what you've done! You've made me the laughingstock of the island!"

Alvin shook his head. "I have merely turned you into what you really are," he said. "From now on, everyone will know that a Doubt is actually a very small thing that should not bother us at all."

When the other members of the rescue party reached the top of the mountain, they were overjoyed with Alvin's victory. The Common Good wanted to carry the hero down the mountain on his shoulders, but the boy insisted that Dr. Cranshaw be carried down instead. The old scientist at first refused, but Alvin knew that Dr. Cranshaw was still in a weakened condition from his ordeal. Finally, after much persuasion, the old scientist relented.

The group stayed in the mountain regions for several weeks, mapping the area and exploring the countryside. At first, Dr. Cranshaw was too weak to do much traveling and stayed close to the safari camp. That meant Alvin was entrusted to take care of much of the exploring. After a few days, the old scientist's strength returned and he was once again able to take command of the safari. However, he never forgot how Alvin had conquered the Doubt, and the feat gave him new respect for the young explorer.

At last, the exploring was finished and the safari made its way back through the forest to the house in the clearing. The return journey was not without its dangers and hardships, but the travelers returned safe and sound.

It was a triumphant day when the expedition entered the clearing. News of Alvin's great victory over the Doubt had already traveled back, mainly due to the fleet-footed work of the Running Commentary, who bellowed out the story to everyone he ran into. As the safari strode through the clearing, the members were greeted with a rousing welcome.

The Appropriate Gesture stepped forth and presented each member with two empty glasses of planter's punch and four slices of bread with nothing in between.

The Glowing Report, accompanied by the Small Wonder, greeted the travelers with the grandest glow of his career—a dazzling glare that spread across half the island.

The Bitter Grudge and the Purple Rage had suspended their hatred for a day so that they could be on hand to cheer the explorers.

Even the Ugly Rumor had temporarily given

up his awful gossiping in order to shout his welcome from a nearby tree stump.

The greatest reception of all, of course, was tendered by the Standing Ovation, whose clapping was so thunderous that it rocked the trees and nearly caused the Bitter Grudge and the Purple Rage to fall off their perches.

Alvin was truly impressed by the magnificent welcome, but he was not at all prepared for what he heard next.

"Alvin!" the creatures all cried. "Alvin! Alvin! Alvin!"

Dr. Cranshaw nudged the young explorer. "They want you to take a bow," he said. "Go ahead, my boy. You deserve it."

Alvin, who had always been taught to behave modestly, tried to ignore the outcry. He truly felt that he had done nothing extraordinary and that the other members of the safari had contributed just as much. But the shouting continued, and finally the young explorer consented to take a bow.

This was greeted with a tremendous final cheer by the onlookers with even Dr. Cranshaw and the other members of the expedition joining in.

Alvin could scarcely believe his ears. "How wonderful it has all been," he said to himself as the roar echoed through the clearing. "How wonderful, indeed."